# Art

## Contents

 **Look and put the sticker.**

pens

paper

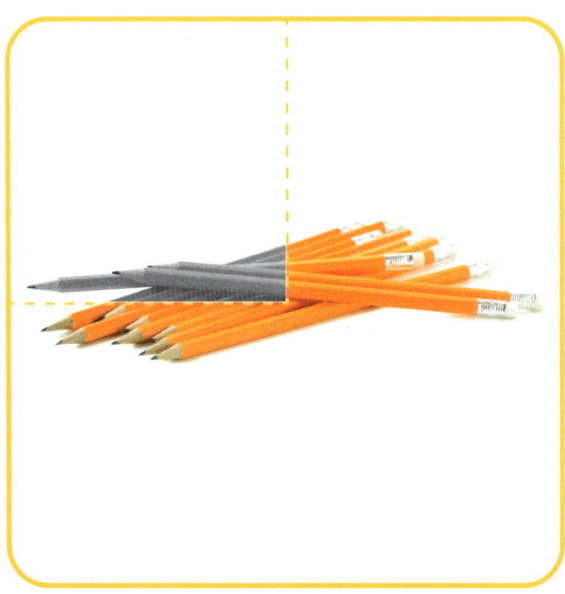

pencils

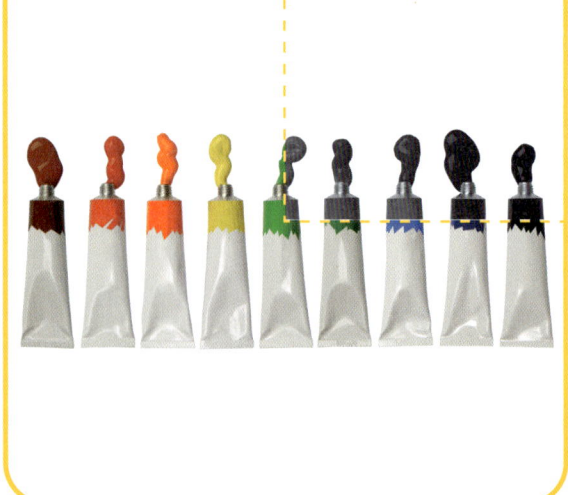

paint

 **Put sticker on the word.**

Do you have paper ?

Yes, I do.

 **Ask and say.**

**Color and say.**

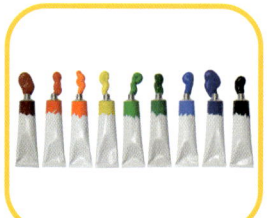

paint

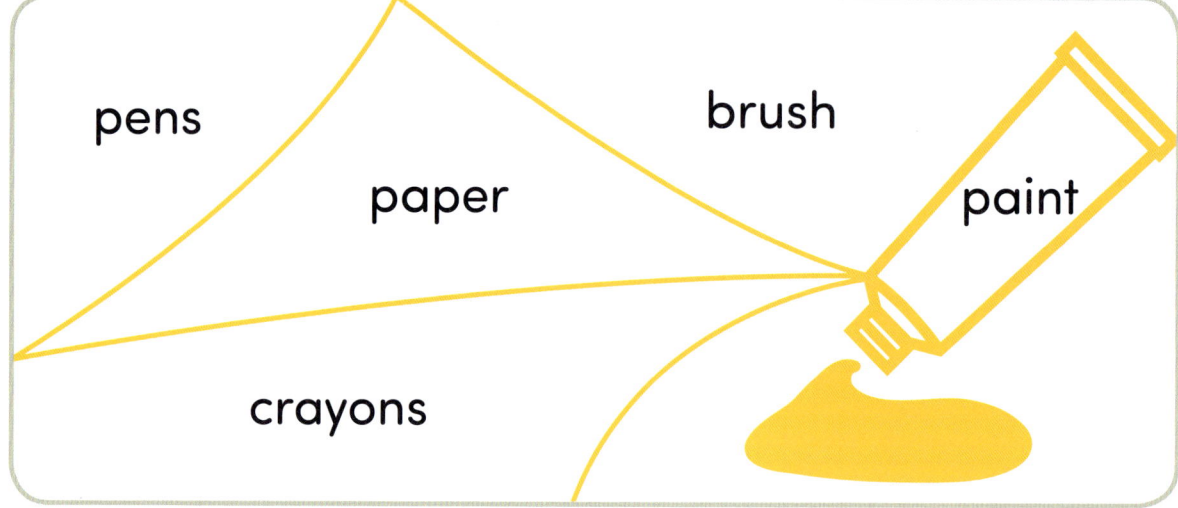

pens

brush

paper

paint

crayons

paper

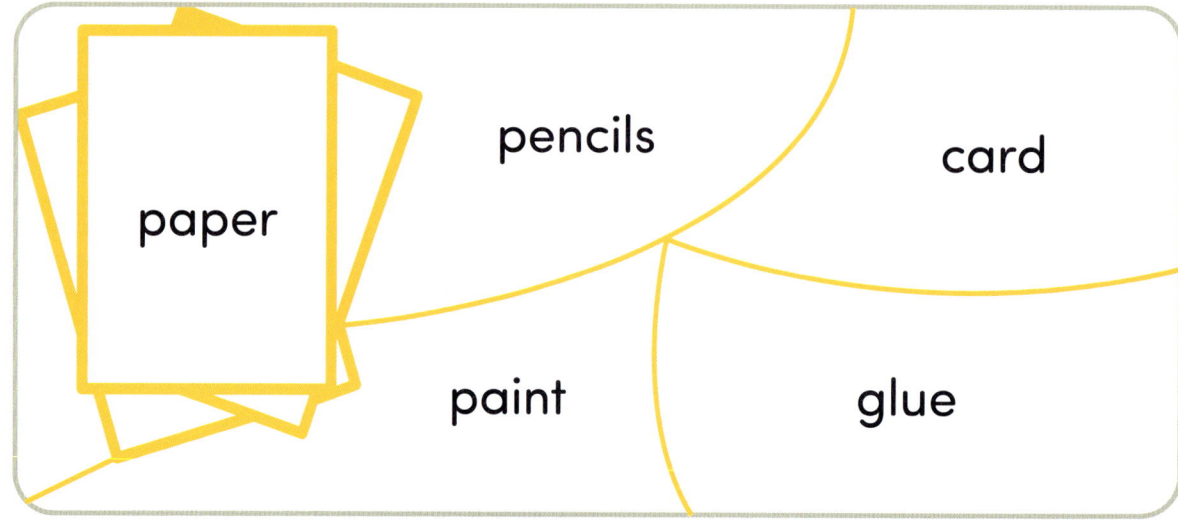

pencils

card

paper

paint

glue

 **Look and put the sticker.**

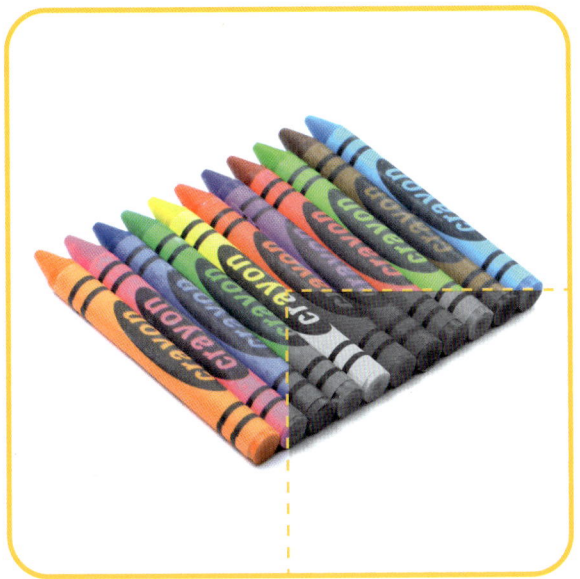

crayons

brush

card

glue

 **Put sticker on the word.**

Do you have crayons ?

Yes, I do.

 **Ask and say.**

**paper**

**crayons**

**Find and circle.**

brush

crayons

 **Make pictures.**

| glue | paper |
|:---:|:---:|
| **paint** | **brush** |

| pencils | card |
|---------|------|
| crayons | pens |